The Rosary of Our Lady of Sorrows

A Guide with Meditations

For K.J. and other mothers that share her sorrow.

"Come, all who pass by the way, pay attention and see: Is there any pain like my pain, which has been ruthlessly inflicted upon me, (Lam 1:12).

†Imprimatur Daniel Cardinal DiNardo
Archbishop Galveston-Houston 2/11/21.

PROMISES FOR DEVOTION TO OUR LADY'S SORROWS:

St. Alphonsus Liguori, in his book *The Glories of Mary* mentioned a revelation in which St. John the Evangelist saw both Our Lord and His Blessed Mother after her assumption into Heaven. He heard Mary ask Jesus for some special grace to all those who are devoted to her sorrows (i). Christ promised the four following special graces:

That those before death who invoked the divine Mother in the name of her sorrows should obtain true repentance of all their sins.

That He would protect all who have this devotion in their tribulations, and that He would protect them especially at the hour of their death.

1

That He would impress upon their minds the remembrance of His Passion, and that they should have their reward for in heaven.

That He would commit such devout clients to the hands of Mary, with the power to dispose of them in whatever manner she might please, and to obtain for them all the graces she might desire.

For her part, Our Blessed Mother revealed to St. Bridget of Sweden that she grants the following seven graces to the souls who honor her daily by saying seven Hail Mary's while meditating on her tears and sorrows:

"I will grant peace to their families."

"They will be enlightened about the divine Mysteries."

"I will console them in their pains, and I will accompany them in their work."

"I will give them as much as they ask for as long as it does not oppose the adorable will of my divine Son or the sanctification of their souls."

"I will defend them in their spiritual battles with the infernal enemy and I will protect them at every instant of their lives."

"I will visibly help them at the moment of their death--they will see the face of their mother."

"I have obtained this grace from my divine Son, that those who propagate this devotion to my tears and dolores will be taken directly from this earthly life to eternal happiness, since all their sins will be

3

forgiven, and my Son will be their eternal consolation and joy."

Background on the Rosary

of Our Lady of Sorrows:

The rosary Our Lady of Sorrows was first used in the city of Florence Italy by a group of devout merchants that were interested in a life of penance. Around the year 1240 they withdrew from the world and eventually were formed into the Servite Order who devoted themselves to Our Lady of Sorrow with this rosary. The seven sorrows of Mary are taken from scripture and trace the life of Our Lady from the presentation to Our Lord being laid in the tomb. In our own times Our Blessed Mother has come to us and urged that we employ this devotion with sincerity and a will to repent and return to God.

On July 2, 2001, the Holy See released the declaration approving the apparitions of Our Lady at Kibeho Rwanda. The apparitions began in 1981 at a boarding school for girls and encouraged repentance, prayer from the heart and sincere devotion. On May 15, 1982 Our Lady related that *"No one gets to heaven without suffering...The Son of Mary is never separated from suffering."* Civil war erupted in Rwanda in 1990 and one million people were slaughtered in a genocidal frenzy that was predicted by Our Lady in the 1980's. In 1982 Our Lady came to plead with people and related that if her instructions were followed the death seen by the visionaries could be avoided. On May 31, 1982, Our Lady said to Marie Claire: ***"What I ask of you is repentance. If you recite this chaplet, while meditating on it, you will then have the strength to repent.***

Today, many people do not know any more how to ask forgiveness. They nail again the Son of God to the Cross. So, I wanted to come and recall it to you, especially here in Rwanda, for here I have still found humble people, who are not attached to wealth nor money." Our Lady asked us to recite this chaplet every day if we can, but especially Fridays, September 14, the feast of the Holy Cross; and on September 15, the feast of Our Lady of Seven Sorrows. She also stated that she did not just come for Rwanda, or Africa but when she comes to speak to us her words are for the entire world (ii).

Our Lord was many things to many people: presumed political leader, prophet, healer, messiah, Lord and God-Man. To His mother He was always one thing: her little boy, her heart, her purpose in life and gift from God.

As one ponders the seven sorrows of this devotion it is important not only to emphasize with the suffering that any mother would have at the sight of her son beaten, bloody and slowly dying, but to realize that just as Our Lord sacrificed and suffered for us, so did his mother.

She was born without the stain of original sin and never committed a mortal sin. Thus, both she and her Son were innocent victims of all the sin that will ever be. His passion was the giving of his life for the world and her task was to give her son back to God. One can imagine her quietly smiling to herself when others would speak of the wisdom that came from his lips and the miracles done by his hands in His public ministry. Quietly smiling and thinking, "That's my little boy, my son." Being free from sin, the great love between the most sacred heart and immaculate heart had to be the most pure and intense ever. Such great love could only result in the deepest heart break on the day of Our Lord's crucifixion. On that day, the immaculate heart of our mother and the Sacred Heart of Jesus would ache beyond human understanding. Our Lord had to bear immeasurable pain on every level and the blessed mother incalculable sorrow in her grief. Our Lord is pleased when we reflect on the sorrow and pain of his mother and our lady is moved when we meditate on the Passion of her Son.

The Catechism of the Church states:
"Mary's role in the Church is inseparable from her union with Christ and flows directly from it. This union of the mother with the Son in the work of salvation is made manifest from the time of Christ's virginal conception up to his death; it is made

*manifest above all at the hour of his
Passion: Thus, the Blessed Virgin advanced
in her pilgrimage of faith, and faithfully
persevered in her union with her Son unto
the cross. There she stood, in keeping with
the divine plan, enduring with her only
begotten Son the intensity of his suffering,
joining herself with his sacrifice in her
mother's heart, and lovingly consenting to
the immolation of this victim, born of her: to
be given, by the same Christ Jesus dying on
the cross, as a mother to his disciple, with
these words: 'Woman, behold your son
(iii)."*

Opening Prayers of the Rosary

To Our Lady of Sorrows:

I offer you this rosary Lord for your greater
glory, my own conversion and that of the

world through your Son, my God, and savior Jesus Christ. May I please increase in my love of you and my fellows as I accompany my holy mother in the sorrows of her earthly life; grow in my appreciation of the price paid for my salvation in precious blood; and come to prefer death over ever seriously offending You again. As I attempt to console our blessed mother, may I appreciate more how much your Sacred Heart and her immaculate heart suffer due to sin and how much rejoicing there is in heaven at the conversion of a single soul. Amen.

Lord, I am sorry for my sins. In choosing to do what is wrong and failing to do what is good, I not only dread the loss of heaven and the reality of hell, but I offend you who I

10

can only rightly love, honor, and obey above all else. I hope that, with the continued help of your grace and strength to confess and do penance for my sin, continue to amend my life, and avoid sin and the occasion of it. Lord Jesus Christ Son of a living God have mercy on me a sinner. Amen.

How to Pray the Rosary

of Our Lady of Sorrows

3x Hail Mary for the tears shed by our blessed mother.

O, Lord come to my assistance. O, God make haste to help me.

Glory be to the Father, Son and Holy Spirit as it was in the beginning is now and ever shall be a world without end. Amen.

The prophecy of Simeon:

"…Simeon blessed them and said to Mary his mother, "Behold, this child is destined for the fall and rise of many in Israel, and to be a sign that will be contradicted (and you yourself a sword will pierce) so that the thoughts of many hearts may be revealed (Lk 2: 34-35)."

Sorrowful mother, I imagine you going to the Temple in joy to present your son with St. Joseph. Once there, you encounter Simeon who predicts that, not only will your infant child be rejected, you also will suffer for the sake of doing God's will. How shocked you must have been to hear this proclamation. Contrasted with the news of Gabriel that your son would ascend to the throne of his father David, pondering the predictions of Simeon must have caused a pang in your maternal heart. Pray for me sorrowful mother that when God's will causes my heart to break, I will have the faith He will make it whole again.

1x Our Father & 7x Hail Mary.

Mary, conceived without sin, pray for us; give us a deep appreciation of your Son and His sacrifice.

The flight to Egypt:

"…the angel of the Lord appeared to Joseph in a dream and said, "Rise, take the child and his mother, flee to Egypt, and stay there until I tell you. Herod is going to search for the child to destroy him." Joseph rose and took the child and his mother by night and departed for Egypt. He stayed there until the death of Herod, that what the Lord had said through the prophet might be fulfilled, "Out of Egypt I called my son (Mt 2: 13-15)."

Sorrowful mother, I imagine how much you must have feared for your new, small family as you fled into the unknown due to St. Joseph's dream. How difficult it must have been, after being the subject of judgement, gossip and ignorant criticisms having been found pregnant out of wedlock, you and your small family were uprooted from all things familiar to protect your infant child. Incomprehensible was the diabolical wrath

14

of Herod toward your perfect, innocent baby. A child so small, and yet, the One who framed the universe. Pray for me sorrowful mother, that I may always place God and his kingdom first above all else.

1x Our Father& 7x Hail Mary.

Mary, conceived without sin, pray for us; give us a deep appreciation of your Son and his sacrifice.

The finding of the child Jesus at the Temple:

"After three days they found him in the temple, sitting in the midst of the teachers, listening to them and asking them questions, and all who heard him were astounded at his understanding and his answers. When his parents saw him, they were astonished, and his mother said to him, "Son, why have you done this to us? Your father and I have been looking for you with great anxiety (Lk 2: 46-48)."

Sorrowful mother, I imagine your heart dropping in your chest at the realization that your son could not be found. How frantic and desperate you and St. Joseph must have been not to find him. Fears that he was hurt, or evil befalling him fueled the panic. Perhaps, being of age, he had chosen to begin the Father's work. What relief and consternation you must have had to find him well and in eager discourse with elders at the Temple. Pray for me sorrowful mother, that when all seems lost, I will have the faith that your Divine Son is not lost, but I still need to seek Him.

1x Our Father & 7x Hail Mary.

Mary, conceived without sin, pray for us; give us a deep appreciation of your Son and his sacrifice.

Our blessed mother meets Jesus on the way to Calvary:

"A large crowd of people followed Jesus, including many women who mourned and lamented him (Lk. 23: 27)."

Sorrowful mother, I find it difficult to imagine or comprehend your seeing your precious son so savagely beaten, bloody, stumbling, and falling under the weight of the cross. When he was a child you could

17

pick him up, dust him off and give him a kiss to ease his pain. Now as you see the child you raised to manhood wounded and subject to the jeers of the crowd, I can only imagine how powerless you felt to witness this horror. In your heart I believe you would be willing to suffer in your Son's place just as he was enduring his suffering for me and all humanity. Women who were total strangers were bereft in empathy to see what had been done to your Son. Pray for me sorrowful mother, that when I fall, I can rise again in your Son's grace and under your loving eye.

1x Our Father & 7x Hail Mary.

Mary, conceived without sin, pray for us; give us a deep appreciation of your Son and his sacrifice.

Jesus suffers and dies on the cross:

"Standing by the cross of Jesus were his mother and his mother's sister, Mary the wife of Clopas, and Mary of Magdala. When Jesus saw his mother and the disciple there whom he loved, he said to his mother, 'Woman, behold, your son.' Then he said to the disciple, 'Behold, your mother.' And from that hour the disciple took her into his home. After this, aware that everything was now finished, in order that the scripture might be fulfilled, Jesus said, 'I thirst'...When Jesus had taken the wine, he said, 'It is finished.' And bowing his head, he

handed over the spirit (Jn. 19: 25-28 &
30)."

Sorrowful mother, I cannot imagine grief
and despair you must have felt at the foot
of the cross watching your son slowly die
in such agony. So great is your love, you
were willing to witness what no mother
should have to see. The pain must have
cut to your very soul as you saw your
only son beaten and pierced upon the
cross. How you must have winced as the
nails were driven into his hands and feet.
The horror and trauma of the moment
must have led you to be oblivious to your
surroundings as you were focused on
your son and the increasing weight in

your heart. Sorrowful mother pray for me that every day that I am grateful for the gift of my life--a life given to me in your Son's sacrifice.

1x Our Father & 7x Hail Mary.

Mary, conceived without sin, pray for us; give us a deep appreciation of your Son and his sacrifice.

Jesus is taken down from the cross:

"Nicodemus, the one who had first come to him at night, came bringing a mixture of myrrh and aloes weighing about one hundred pounds. They took the body of Jesus and bound it with burial cloths along with the spices, according to the Jewish burial custom, (Jn. 19: 39-40)."

21

Sorrowful mother, the tears of joy shed while holding your son at his birth have turned to rivers of deep sorrow. No mother expects to hold the lifeless body of their own child. How it must have torn you to the core when the soldier thrust his lance into the destroyed body of your child. Holding that body now, I imagine your feelings could only be expressed in wordless sobs.

1x Our Father & 7x Hail Mary.

Mary conceived without sin, pray for us; give us a deep appreciation of your Son and his sacrifice.

Jesus is laid in the tomb:

"It was the day of preparation, and the sabbath was about to begin. The women

who had come from Galilee with him
followed behind, and when they had seen
the tomb and the way in which his body was
laid in it, they returned and prepared
perfumes and oils (Lk 23: 54-56)."

I imagine you must have been despondent as
the stone to the tomb was rolled into place.
The finality of that moment was the ultimate
twist in the sword piercing your heart. The
shock and trauma of the day and watching
your son slowly die had taken its toll. I see
sadness clinging to you like a shawl draped
over your sunken shoulders. Your head cast
down, staring at the ground. I can envision
you slowly walking away from the tomb
with St. John and in silence. A blank
expression on your tear-stained face. Your

eyes now dry and red having exhausted all the tears of your maternal heart.

1x Our Father &7x Hail Mary.

Mary, conceived without sin, pray for us; give us a deep appreciation of your Son and his sacrifice.

Closing Prayer

I thank you Lord that I am better acquainted with you, your mother, and the price paid to give me life. I will never be able to fully appreciate how much you both have done for me while I am on earth. I do praise, glorify, and bless the Eternal Father for sending you, Lord Jesus. I praise, glorify, and bless you Lord for your holy life, passion, cross and resurrection by which you

have conquered the world, sin, and death. I
praise glorify and bless your holy mother
and St. Joseph for saying "Yes…" to God. I
am Grateful for the Living, Holy Spirit
which you have sent to guide us and to
renew the face of the earth. Amen.

Litany of Our Lady of Sorrows

Lord, have mercy on us.
Christ, have mercy on us.
Lord, have mercy on us.

Christ, hear us.
Christ, graciously hear us.
God, the Father of heaven,
Have mercy on us.
God the Son, Redeemer of the world,
Have mercy on us.
God the Holy Ghost,
Have mercy on us.
Holy Mary, Mother of God,
pray for us.

Holy Virgin of virgins,
pray for us.
Mother of the Crucified,
pray for us.
Sorrowful Mother,
pray for us.
Mournful Mother,
pray for us.
Sighing Mother,
pray for us.
Afflicted Mother,
pray for us.
Foresaken Mother,
pray for us.
Desolate Mother,
pray for us.

Mother most sad,
pray for us.
Mother set around with anguish,
pray for us.
Mother overwhelmed by grief,
pray for us.
Mother transfixed by a sword,
pray for us.
Mother crucified in thy heart,
pray for us.
Mother bereaved of thy Son,
pray for us.
Sighing Dove,
pray for us.
Mother of Dolors,
pray for us.

Fount of tears,
pray for us.
Sea of bitterness,
pray for us.
Field of tribulation,
pray for us.
Mass of suffering,
pray for us.
Mirror of patience,
pray for us.
Rock of constancy,
pray for us.
Remedy in perplexity,
pray for us.
Joy of the afflicted,
pray for us.

Light of Confessors,
pray for us.
Pearl of Virgins,
pray for us.
Comfort of Widows,
pray for us.
Joy of all Saints,
pray for us.
Queen of thy Servants,
pray for us.
Holy Mary, who alone art unexampled,
pray for us.

Pray for us, most Sorrowful Virgin,
That we may be made worthy of the
promises of Christ.

O God, in whose Passion, according to the prophecy of Simeon, a sword of grief pierced through the most sweet soul of Thy glorious Blessed Virgin Mother Mary: grant that we, who celebrate the memory of her Seven Sorrows, may obtain the happy effect of Thy Passion, Who lives and reigns world without end. Amen.
Say the Creed, Hail Holy Queen and 3x Hail Mary.

Pope Pius VII 1809 While under captivity of Napoleon.

Prayer of Maximillian Kolbe Recited Daily by St. John Paul II

Immaculate conception, Mary, my Mother, live in me, act in me. Speak in and through me. Think your thoughts in my mind. Love, through my heart. Give me your dispositions and feelings. Teach, lead, and guide me to Jesus. Correct, enlighten and expand my thoughts behavior. Possess my soul. Take over my entire personality and life. Replace it with yourself. Incline me to constant adoration and thanksgiving. Pray in me and through me. Let me live in you and keep me in this union always. Amen.

Consecration of the whole world and peoples to the Immaculate Heart of Mary

May 13, 1982

*On Thursday, 13 May 1982, after the concelebrated Mass in Fatima, Pope John Paul II made the following act of consecration of the modern world to Our Lady of Fatima.*iv

1. "We have recourse to your protection, holy Mother of God."

As I utter the words of this antiphon with which the Church of Christ has prayed for centuries, I find myself today in this place chosen by you, O Mother, and by you particularly loved.

I am here, united with all the Pastors of the Church in that particular bond whereby we constitute a body and a college, just as Christ desired the Apostles to be in union with Peter.

In the bond of this union, I utter the words of the present Act, in which I wish to include, once more, the hopes and anxieties of the Church in the modern world.

Forty years ago and again ten years later, your servant Pope Pius XII, having before his eyes the painful experience of the human family, entrusted and consecrated to your Immaculate Heart the whole world, especially the peoples for which you had particular love and solicitude.

This world of individuals and nations I too have before my eyes today, as I renew the entrusting and consecration carried out by my Predecessor in the See of Peter: the world of the second millennium that is drawing to a close, the modern world, our world today!

The Church, mindful of the Lord's words: "Go... and make disciples of all nations... and lo, I am with you always, to the close of the age" (Mt 28:19-20), renewed, at the Second Vatican Council, her awareness of her mission in this world.

And therefore, O Mother of individuals and peoples, you who "know all their sufferings-and their hopes", you who have a mother's awareness of all the struggles between good and evil, between light and darkness, which afflict the modern world, accept the cry which we, as though moved by the Holy Spirit, address directly to your Heart. Embrace, with the love of the Mother and Handmaid, this human world of ours, which we entrust and consecrate to you, for we are full of disquiet for the earthly and eternal destiny of individuals and peoples.

In a special way we entrust and consecrate to you those individuals and nations which particularly need to be entrusted and consecrated.

"We have recourse to your protection, holy Mother of God: reject not the prayers we send up to you in our necessities. Reject them not! Accept our humble trust-and our act of entrusting!

2. "For God so loved the world that he gave his only Son, that whoever believes in him should not perish but have eternal life" (Jn 3:16).

It was precisely by reason of this love that the Son of God consecrated himself for all mankind: "And for their sake I consecrate myself, that they also may be consecrated in truth" (In 17:19).

By reason of that consecration the disciples of all ages are called to spend themselves for the salvation of the world, and to supplement Christ's afflictions for the sake of his body, that is the Church (cf. 2 Cor 12:15; Col 1:24).

Before you, Mother of Christ, before your Immaculate Heart, I today, together with the whole Church, unite myself with our Redeemer in this his consecration for the world and for people, which only in his divine Heart has the power to obtain pardon and to secure reparation.

The power of this consecration lasts for all time and embraces all individuals, peoples and nations. It overcomes every evil that the spirit of darkness is able to awaken, and has in fact awakened in our times, in the heart of man and in his history.

The Church, the Mystical Body of Christ, unites herself, through the service of

Peter's successor, to this consecration by our Redeemer.

Oh, how deeply we feel the need for consecration on the part of humanity and of the world-our modern world-in union with Christ himself! The redeeming work of Christ, in fact, must be shared in by the world by means of the Church.

Oh, how pained we are by all the things in the Church and in each one of us that are opposed to holiness and consecration! How pained we are that the invitation to repentance, to conversion, to prayer, has not met with the acceptance that it should have received!

How pained we are that many share so coldly in Christ's work of Redemption! That "what is lacking in Christ's afflictions" is so insufficiently completed in our flesh.

And so, blessed be all those souls that obey the call of eternal Love! Blessed be all those who, day after day, with undiminished generosity accept your invitation, O Mother, to do what your Jesus tells them (cf. Jn 2:5) and give the

Church and the world a serene testimony of lives inspired by the Gospel.

Above all blessed be you, the Handmaid of the Lord, who in the fullest way obey the divine call!

Hail to you, who are wholly united to the redeeming consecration of your Son!

Mother of the Church! Enlighten the People of God along the paths of faith, of hope and love! Help us to live with the whole truth of the consecration of Christ for the entire human family of the modern world.

3. In entrusting to you, O Mother, the world, all individuals and peoples, we also entrust to you the consecration itself, for the world's sake, placing it in your motherly Heart.

Oh, Immaculate Heart! Help us to conquer the menace of evil, which so easily takes root in the hearts of the people of today, and whose immeasurable effects already weigh down upon our modern world and seem to block the paths towards the future!

From famine and war, deliver us.

From nuclear war, from incalculable self-destruction, from every kind of war, deliver us.

From sins against the life of man from its very beginning, deliver us. From hatred and from the demeaning of the dignity of the children of God, deliver us.

From every kind of injustice in the life of society, both national and international, deliver us.

From readiness to trample on the commandments of God, deliver us.

From attempts to stifle in human hearts the very truth of God, deliver us.

From sins against the Holy Spirit, deliver us, deliver us.

Accept, O Mother of Christ, this cry laden with the sufferings of all individual human beings, laden with the sufferings of whole societies.

Let there be revealed, once more. in the history of the world your infinite power of merciful Love. May it put a stop to evil. May it transform consciences. May your Immaculate Heart reveal for all the light of Hope

Endnotes:

i-Our Catholic Prayers. (2018). *Promises of the Rosary of Our Lady of Sorrows*. Retrieved on 2/24/19 from: from https://www.ourcatholicprayers.com/Sorrow ful-mothers-devotion-promises.html.

iii-*Catechism of the Catholic Church*. 2nd ed. Vatican: Librereia Editrice Vaticana. (2012). Print. Article 9, Paragraph 6:964.

iii-Tardif, Therese. (10/1/2001). *Messages of Our Lady of Sorrows in Kibeho, Rwanda.* Retrieved on 1/24/19 from: https://www.michaeljournal.org/articles/rom an-catholic-church/item/messages-of-our-lady-of-sorrows-in-kibeho-rwanda.

iv-St. John Paul II. (5.13.1982).
Consecration of the World on May 13, 1982 to the Immactualte Heart of Mary. Retrieved 11/15/20 from:
https://www.catholicculture.org/culture/library/view.cfm?recnum=631.

Printed in Great Britain
by Amazon

85880179R00032